PRODUCTIVITY 23 POWERFUL TIPS

PRODUCTIVITY

23

POWERFUL

TIPS

PRODUCTIVITY 23 POWERFUL TIPS

PRODUCTIVITY 23 POWERFUL TIPS

INDEX

1. Set a game plan!

2. Reduction of distractions

3. What should you do first?

4. Exercise of self-discipline

5. You can do the impossible

6. Increased motivation

7. Don't let setbacks get you down!

8. Be goal-oriented

9. Take care of yourself!

10. Why being organized is essential

11. When you need to delegate

12. Avoiding exhaustion

13. Supplies are a factor

14. A positive mental framework

15. Resisting negativity

16. The tasks for your goal

17. About your co-workers and employees

18. Personal Stimulus

19. Resist spreading yourself too thin

20. Why you need to de-stress

21. Establishing and classifying your priorities

22. Exercise good communication skills

23. Strategies are appropriate everywhere!

1. Set a game plan!

One factor that all successful people have in common is effective time management. You may prefer to call it structure, setting the task, or a game plan. Any word or term that works for you is fine. As long as you take it seriously and put it into practice, you're creating one of the basic principles of productivity.

It may be a good idea to think about this, and why this factor is so essential to success. Perhaps you can start by thinking about the opposite: ways that don't work. Even if you have a very small task to complete, if you don't manage your time properly, you may do it too late or not at all. You may be working to a deadline or have a task that you don't have a specific time frame for completing. If you don't have a game plan to do it, the results won't be satisfactory. While delay and loss of time impede productivity, lack of effective time management can be just as destructive.

Increasing your productivity and getting things done means having a good game plan. First, you need to know exactly what needs to be done. Second, even if you don't have a specific deadline, you also need to decide when it should be done. The third step is to get on with the task of doing it.

You want to meet your goals whether they are short term or long term. You also want to be proud and satisfied with the results. When you are not content to simply "go with the flow" and instead take your game plan seriously every step of the way, success, pride and satisfaction are almost guaranteed.

Structure and time management can be easy if they have been a part of your life. If you are not used to these concepts, now is the time to implement them in your daily life. Whether you are setting up your own business, working for someone else, or if your job is taking care of your family, you will get a lot of benefits and rewards from establishing a good game plan.

If you have ever felt that there are not enough hours in a day to do everything you need to do, this will be a very positive step for you. You will be pleasantly surprised at how much you can accomplish. With a game plan, you may find yourself doing more each

 PRODUCTIVITY 23 POWERFUL TIPS

day than you normally accomplish in a week. Not only will you be more productive, but achieving each goal will be much easier.

2. Reduction of distractions

There are few things that block productivity as quickly and safely as distractions. When you can't concentrate and focus properly, you can't get things done. Even if you do accomplish something, it can be stressful and frustrating. Whether you're at work, in school, or in your field, reducing the distractions that influence your ability to be productive will help you get more done.

There are two key points to keep in mind when planning to reduce distractions in your environment. The first point is what works for you and what works for someone else may be completely different. The second point is that unless you've examined your habits, you may not be 100 percent sure about which habits are most effective for you. The good news is that it doesn't take much time or effort to consider how your habits are affecting your productivity, and to begin adjusting them accordingly.

If you're like most people these days, multi-tasking has become part of your everyday life and your everyday vocabulary. There may be a number of things you need to do in a day, and you may be doing them simultaneously. If you overdo it with multitasking, there can be two consequences. You may not do everything; or it may go on too long and not have satisfactory results.

The same goes for distractions. Trying to do a

job, and doing it correctly and well, will not yield satisfactory results if you allow distractions to get in the way. Working while listening to music, watching TV or chatting on the phone is not limited to teenagers. Many adults do these things in their home offices, and even in an office that is occupied by other people.

They may help your concentration, but they can just as easily ruin your focus and distract you from what you're doing. Being more productive requires some analysis of your habits. You can turn off some or all of these distractions and see if you can focus better on the task at hand. You may find that you can do the job better, faster, and more effectively without any distractions. On the other hand, you may find that one of these factors actually helps your concentration.

While finding what works for you is easy if you work on your own, it can be a little more complicated if you work with others. Coworkers who constantly use their phones, visit or listen to their radios near their work space may distract you from concentrating on your work. If you approach them politely, this may be all it takes to reduce the distractions so you can concentrate on your work.

3. What should you do first?

If you think about when you were in school, you can remember that teachers told you that the best way to tackle homework and other projects was to do the hardest task first. They may also have advised you to tackle the task you disliked most before continuing. This same approach can greatly improve your productivity today.

When you're getting ready to start a new day at work, try to begin implementing this approach. Instead of starting with a task you like, or a task you find easy, start with one you don't like or that seems pretty difficult.

At the end of the day, you may be pleasantly surprised by what you've accomplished. You will also feel that the day has gone much more smoothly.

One reason for this is that you will have more energy at the beginning of your work day. When you devote this energy to the more difficult or unpleasant tasks, you will not feel so exhausted or frustrated in doing them. A second reason is that if you start with tasks you enjoy, you often find yourself looking ahead to those you don't like in a very negative way. Instead of enjoying the easier tasks while you're doing them, you're dreading the ones that lie ahead. When you do the harder ones first, not only will you have more energy left for the rest of the day, but you will also appreciate the other tasks more when you do them.

This approach will increase your productivity. When you don't view your work day as a long, uphill battle, you will achieve more. Getting the tasks you don't like first, early in the day, will generate better results with all your tasks. Not only will you achieve more, but you will be much more satisfied with the outcome of each task.

While it is only human nature to want to do what you like first, having the most difficult things on the horizon can slow you down and drain your energy. If you want to be more productive and achieve the best results in everything you do, follow the advice of your school teachers and tackle the toughest jobs first. Your productivity will increase and you will end each day with a refreshing sense of accomplishment.

4. Exercise of self-discipline

Self-discipline is an essential factor for productivity and success. Without it, one becomes lazy, unmotivated and dependent on others. Lack of self-discipline also makes it difficult to deal with employees, bosses or co-workers.

Exercising self-discipline means, in an old-fashioned way, getting down to business. You need to know what needs to be done, when it needs to be done, and how to do it. Good self-discipline includes a basic schedule or framework of what must be accomplished within a specific period of time.

However, being too rigid with self-discipline does not increase productivity. It may even decrease it. If you don't allow yourself any breaks during the workday, or there is no margin for error, the expectations you are setting for yourself are too rigid. Instead of doing more, or doing more in a shorter period of time, it can make you feel frustrated with your tasks and your work.

If you learned self-discipline early in life, you probably won't have any difficulties now. On the other hand, if your school years and family life were too rigid, or if little was expected of you, this is a good time to develop the habit. You may have managed to slip through your early years without a good sense of self-discipline, but it will be a hindrance to your career.

A good way to begin cultivating self-discipline is to recognize what you are responsible for. You can start by taking responsibility for doing the job correctly and on time. If this is a relatively new concept for you, you must also recognize that mistakes occur and be able to correct them without undue frustration.

Exercising self-discipline also includes not getting sidetracked by distractions and time-wasting activities. While you may need and deserve a short break during your workday, you can't take it away from your work. When you have developed the habit of self-discipline, completing tasks will be easier. They will be done well and on time. You will increase your productivity and it will help you get much closer to success.

5. You can do the impossible

If you have ever had to complete so many different tasks, or tasks that seemed to be beyond your capabilities, you know what it is like to feel that it is impossible. When these types of tasks are within your range of responsibility, there are some positive ways you can approach them. You may find that you can really do the impossible.

Sometimes you may see tasks as impossible because you are overwhelmed by the amount you need to do in a short period of time. Even if each one is quite simple, they can add up to a mountain of work that you cannot reasonably expect to finish. This can happen. It takes on more than you can handle, or when unexpected "surprises" arise without proper preparation.

A positive approach to the above situation is to be reasonable about what you can do at first. If you take on too much it is because of issues such as:

- A financial need.
- Trying to look good for your boss.
- Overcoming a co-worker.

Assessing your abilities beforehand can eliminate this problem. An effective approach to this situation is to learn to prioritize. If an unexpected task or project comes up while you're dealing with your other tasks, you need to decide which tasks need to be completed immediately and which can wait until later. In many cases, requesting more time to do everything is a good idea.

Sometimes you may have a project that is really beyond your capabilities. In these cases, the best approach is to recognize your limitations. Depending on the circumstances, you may ask for help or declare that you cannot do it.

Good time management and a clear recognition of your abilities are the keys to doing the impossible. Instead of feeling overwhelmed by work, or stressed by something you are simply unable to do, you will increase your energy and self-esteem. While no one can do everything, and no one can do everything equally well, you will do your best. This, in turn, will reduce the feeling of being overwhelmed and help you be much more productive.

6. Increased motivation

We have all heard people say that they were "not motivated" as an excuse not to do things. In most cases, this is a polite way of saying they are lazy. In the real world, where productivity and success are essential, motivation is a key element. If it doesn't come naturally to you, you can examine ways to increase your own motivation and put it into practice every day.

The more motivated you are, the more you can do. One way you can try to increase your motivation is to enjoy and appreciate your accomplishments. Instead of waiting until you've reached your goal, start by enjoying and appreciating every task you complete along the way. While you shouldn't waste time or get sidetracked, giving yourself a figurative pat on the back for tasks completed well and correctly can be a great way to increase your motivation. You will want to do more; and you will want to continue to excel.

When you do this, you will also help increase your stamina. Instead of feeling overwhelmed by a major goal on the horizon, which can leave you tired and stressed, you can make yourself feel more energetic and better prepared for the next task.

It's easy for a person to lose his or her sense of motivation when he or she feels like they're not accomplishing anything. This can make you feel bad about what you're doing and even make you do less. Fortunately, it's not hard to reverse this pattern and get to the top. When you get used to feeling good about every task you complete and taking pride in each and every accomplishment, you will increase your motivation to do even more and do it better each time.

As your motivation and energy are connected, you will also find that you have much more energy for all the tasks ahead of you. No matter how big your ultimate goal is or how much time and work you need to put in to achieve that particular goal, you will be pleasantly surprised at how much more progress you make. As your motivation and energy increase, you will get more and more. You will see how much productivity you can do every day.

7. Don't let setbacks get you down!

One of the biggest obstacles to productivity is an approach that many people take to setbacks. If you see a setback as a failure, not only can you limit your productivity, but you can also stop yourself from doing something. This is true in any line of work, schooling, or any other area of life. When you see a setback as a failure, you can stop it from continuing. You can achieve less, or you can achieve nothing at all. Setbacks occur in all areas of life. Regardless of the type of work you have, you probably experience them occasionally or on a regular basis. Setbacks can occur from making mistakes, from not being adequately prepared for what you need to do, or from unexpected problems that are not anyone's fault. How you experience and view a setback determines how it will affect you and your productivity.

However, if a setback occurs, there is a perspective that can prevent it from becoming an obstacle and, in fact, increase your productivity. If the setback was due to a mistake on your part, or if it was no one's fault, refusing to see it as a failure is the first step to getting it back on track.

The second step is to see the setback as an opportunity to improve next time. If you have made a mistake in your work, the best approach is to try to correct the mistake and move on. While it's essential that you don't try to hide a mistake, you can't let a mistake stop you. If you don't correct it and move forward, you may find yourself thinking about what happened or becoming obsessed with it. These behaviors are never helpful. Not only will they stop you from doing things, but they will also make you feel bad about yourself. In the worst case, it can make you feel incompetent. This is not the way to do things.

Seeing every setback as a learning experience is a much better approach. You can tell yourself that you are capable of doing better and doing more. As long as you look at setbacks this way, rather than failures, they won't stop you from moving forward. Correct the mistake, learn from it and move on. When you have developed this pattern and make it a regular part of your work life, setbacks will not stand in the way of you being productive.

8. Be goal-oriented

You might be surprised how many people don't know what they're aiming for in their working life. On the other hand, you could be one of those people yourself. If so, now is the time to get your bearings. When you know where you're going, that's one of the most important steps in making sure you get there.

When you're getting ready to go to work in the morning, what's the first thought that comes into your mind about your goal? If you're like a lot of people, you don't think of it in terms of a goal at all. Instead, you may be thinking about how much work you will have to do, or how good the pay will be at the end of the week. If you change your thoughts to a goal, it will be much more productive.

Depending on the nature of your work, goals can take a variety of different forms. You may have something to produce on your own, or you may be part of a team. You can have a very positive sense of self-discipline, or you can work very well as a team player. Whatever the summary of your place in your working life, being goal-oriented will increase your productivity.

Being goal-oriented doesn't have to mean focusing solely on one big achievement. If you start to think of it as a series of small goals, each one you achieve will give you two benefits, which are:

- Being more motivated to continue.
- Being closer to your goal.

Nothing can be achieved overnight. Anything worthwhile requires time, effort and work. When you look at the distance and the steps you must take to get there, you will soon see how much more productive you will be each step of the way. Simply going with the flow and not putting your emphasis on your goals will slow you down. You won't accomplish much if you don't focus on achieving them. When you know where you are going, it is the surest way to know you will get there.

9. Take care of yourself!

If you're like most people, you've probably had the experience of working all night to do something. You may not have slept, or fed, and other important factors in self-care in order to complete a task or meets a deadline. While it is sometimes necessary to do this, neglecting self-care on a regular or frequent basis will be counterproductive. Your health can suffer as long as you don't achieve almost as much as you had hoped.

Taking care of yourself will not only keep you in good health, it will also keep you productive. The person who does not sleep regularly, or who relies on junk food instead of eating nutritious meals, will not be physically or mentally up to the task. While you may think you are giving 100 percent to your job, these unhealthy habits are harmful.

On the other hand, if you get enough sleep on a regular basis and eat a healthy diet, you will have more to give to your work. When you're in top shape, you'll concentrate better, be more alert, and not tire so easily. You'll do better and you'll do more.

If your work day has consisted of many cups of coffee or other artificial energy stimulators, it's time to examine your personal care habits. If you find that you haven't gotten enough sleep and have relied on these products to keep you going, or if you feel that good nutrition has been replaced by junk food and snacks, it's time to evaluate what these habits are doing to your overall health. It's also time to think about the effects it can have on your job.

Although almost everyone is occasionally in the position of skipping a meal or working late at night, if these have become habits for you, it's not likely that they are helping you be more productive. In fact, they're probably holding you back.

Even if you have a fast-paced job with lots of responsibilities and deadlines, neglecting proper self-care is counterproductive. When you start to develop the habit of getting enough sleep and eating a proper diet, you'll do more than just take care of yourself. You will do more and be more satisfied with the results.

10. Why being organized is essential

If you think about it, being organized is one of the most essential factors in being productive. You don't need to be extremely rigid to be organized, but you do need to be aware and conscious of all that your workday entails. Getting things done means getting organized with your time, the supplies and equipment you use, and your expectations.

You can think of someone who is disorganized and how it affects their work. You may rush through the work day from time to time, miss appointments, be unsure of what to accomplish, and be careless with the supplies or equipment you work with during the day. This is a person who doesn't get things done because being disorganized prevents him or her from being productive.

You will be much more successful in a shorter period of time if you are well organized. You can start by making a basic schedule of what to do and when to do it. You can make sure you know in advance where all your supplies are, so you don't waste time looking for something when you need to use it.

Being organized with time and material items is not difficult. However, if you haven't already cultivated this habit, it may take a little practice before you start feeling completely natural. Preparing a summary of your work day will help you get where you need to be and get things done on time. Keeping all your supplies organized and tidy will help you avoid wasting time and feeling frustrated that you can't easily find items when you need them.

When your goal is to increase your productivity, getting things done, getting organized is essential. If you are one of the many people who have not yet developed this positive habit, the results may surprise you. You will soon see that you are achieving much more, doing a better job and ending up with results that are more satisfying. Getting better organized in every aspect of your work life will greatly improve your productivity.

11. When you need to delegate

There are two different types of delegation that are negative. Both can inhibit productivity, rather than increase it. If you recognize some of these factors in your work life, you can begin to change them for better results.

The first negative form of delegation involves the person who wants to do everything himself. While this may sound positive at first, in reality it is not positive at all. The person who insists on doing more work than he or she can reasonably do, or work that he or she is not fully capable of doing on his or her own, not only becomes less productive but also affects the productivity of everyone who counts on him or her to do the job. If you are afraid to ask for help or if you are simply presumptuous, you can hold everyone else up, as well as yourself.

The second negative form of delegation involves the person avoiding his or her own responsibilities. You can ask others to do tasks that you really should be doing yourself. Not only are you not carrying your own weight, but you are taking up other people's valuable time.

Positive delegation makes sense. When you recognize that you cannot do everything, and that you cannot do everything equally well, you are increasing your own productivity as well as the productivity of those around you.

When you have a very large or difficult task or project, asking others to help you do the work and do it faster. Instead of seeing delegation as an admission of weakness or incompetence, you are recognizing the extent of your own role and capabilities. This, in turn, will give others the opportunity to participate and help get the job done.

Delegating in the interest of doing less than you can do, or less than you are reasonably expected to do, is always negative. However, when you are faced with more work than you can reasonably do on your own, or a job you are not able to complete on your own, delegating is the sensible solution. When a job needs to be done, and on time, and well, teamwork will give the best results.

12. Avoiding exhaustion

There is very little that can cause a decrease in productivity as easily as exhaustion. While you may be tempted to believe that devoting every waking moment to working on your job is a good way to get things done, there is one additional factor you may not have considered. When you figuratively take your work home with you, you can increase your risk of burnout and accomplish much less in the long run.

This way of taking your work home does not involve doing essential work during your free time. It involves keeping your work in mind during your off hours. When you are at home or somewhere else other than your workplace, you can easily become overwhelmed by keeping it as your main focus.

During your free hours, you can spend a lot of time thinking about your work. You may worry about whether you will do something on time or the overall quality of your work.

This can lead to being overly stressed, anxious, and overwhelmed. You may feel more fatigued by your work when you are thinking about it and worrying about it than when you are actually doing your job.

If you don't have work to complete after your normal work day, you can avoid burnout by leaving your work at home. Instead of stressing about whatever you need to accomplish the next day, or about the progress you're making with something you're working on, try to learn to put those thoughts and concerns where they belong.

13. Supplies are a factor

You may have heard the old saying that a good worker always takes care of his tools. This is equally relevant whether you work in an office or from home. Keeping all your supplies in excellent working order and easily accessible will make you more productive.

No matter what type of supplies you use during your average workday, neglect can slow you down. You can't do a job effectively if your supplies are broken, damaged or worn out from use. If you try to use supplies that are not in good condition, the quality of your work may suffer. It can take much longer to get things done, and they won't be as good as they could be with supplies that are in the best condition.

Think of it this way: if you are trying to work on a computer that is not up to scratch, or you are using a hand tool that is bent or damaged, or office equipment that stops while you are using it, your productivity can come to a complete halt. You may feel frustrated or angry, and possibly not do the job at all.

When all your supplies, tools and equipment are kept in ideal conditions, they are in better shape to do the job properly. Your work won't be slowed down and you won't run the risk of errors from faulty equipment. Good supplies in good condition mean getting things done and getting the best results.

No matter how much of a hurry you are in to complete a task and end a day's work, taking a few minutes to make sure everything is in good shape will save you time and eliminate unnecessary frustration. You can also replace damaged supplies or equipment as soon as possible. You can take this new positive habit even further by making sure all your supplies and equipment are stored where they belong when you're done using them. These new habits will benefit you, as well as everyone who uses the same supplies and equipment. It will make your work day much smoother and you will be more productive.

When you have time off, develop some positive habits. Learning to relax, participates in healthy recreational activities, and give time and attention to your friends and family will reduce the risk of burnout. Once you have started to develop these habits, it won't take long to see the results.

You will start each new workday feeling physically, emotionally, and mentally refreshed. You will have more to give to your work when it is updated. You will be more motivated, more energetic and more productive.

14. A positive mental framework

Nothing has the power to increase your productivity as surely and easily as a positive mood. While you may not have the time or inclination to repeat affirmations to yourself during the workday, it is essential to recognize that your mindset influences and affects your productivity.

If you have problems in your personal life, the more you are able to keep them out of your workday, the better you will perform. Even if something is especially problematic, you should do everything you can to keep your personal problems separate from your work life. If there's something you need help with, getting it during your free time can keep it from interfering with your work.

On the other hand, if there is something negative in your work life, it should be addressed and dealt with as soon as possible. Feeling overwhelmed, anxious, stressed, or overwhelmed will only slow you down.

The more you can be positive and optimistic, the more you will achieve. Even if you're facing a task that is especially big or difficult, a positive mood can help you accomplish more than you thought you could.

Nothing can be done all at once. Sometimes it takes many small steps to do something. Sometimes mistakes and setbacks occur.

However, when you realize that each step brings you closer to your goal, you are on the right track. When you tell yourself that every small achievement is a goal in itself, you are giving yourself the encouragement and motivation you need for success.

Having a positive state of mind does not come naturally to everyone. If you are one of the many people who have never given it much thought, today is the ideal time to start. A positive state of mind will allow you to feel more confident about yourself and your abilities. Even if self-confidence is a relatively new experience for you, you will be reaping the rewards in no time. You will soon see how important a positive mood is and this will result in you being more satisfied with the results.

15. Resisting negativity

Negativity is a big block to productivity. It also ensures that whatever is done is neither satisfactory nor appreciated. Whether the negativity to be resisted is your own or someone else's, the sooner it is resolved, the sooner it will return to normal.

Negativity can come in many forms, and all of them are counterproductive. Negativity can come in the form of contempt. You may be unsure of your ability to do the job or do it well. If you believe that failure is on the horizon, this is the surest way to make it happen. You can resist the negativity of contempt by reminding yourself of your competence. You may need to practice doing this regularly. When you don't allow a negative light to overshadow your abilities, you will not be able to stop.

Negativity can also come in the form of complaints. Whether you complain about your job or something else in your life, this type of negativity can affect your work. Complaining wears you down and ruins your ability to concentrate properly. When you resist the urge to complain every time you feel like it, you will take steps to keep the negativity out of your work life. Instead of getting tired and cranky from complaining, your energy level will be at its best.

Worry is another form of negativity. It can slow you down and make you less productive. Although it may seem difficult, a good approach is to remember that worrying doesn't accomplish anything. If the issue is something you can resolve, doing it as quickly as possible will reduce your worry. If it can't be addressed immediately, try to forget the concern while you work. You may even need to tell yourself that worrying alone won't solve a problem. This will help you focus and concentrate better.

If you find that your negativity is extreme, asking for outside help may be helpful. You can learn to be in a better state of mind. This is better for your overall health, and also better for your productivity. The more you are able to resist negativity on a regular basis, the more you will achieve.

16. The tasks for your goal

Some people have a habit of seeing their goal as the main thing they need to achieve. They may even see it as the only thing they need to achieve. If this sounds familiar, you are missing out on something very important that can increase your productivity. If you look at each and every task you need to complete to achieve your goal as something very important in yourself, your progress will be much smoother and you will be able to do more.

A good way to think about this is in terms of building a house. If you only think about the whole house, you are missing out on all the steps along the way. There are many steps needed to build a house. None can be omitted or done wrong if you want the house to be strong and in excellent condition when it is finished.

The goals you have in your work life are similar. Regardless of what your particular goal is, there are a number of steps that must be taken to achieve it. For the best possible results, each task requires time, effort, work and concentration.

If you have a very important goal ahead of you, you may be tempted to shorten some of the tasks in between. You may even feel that rushing through your tasks will help you reach your ultimate goal much sooner. This is never a good approach. When you don't do your best on each and every task, no matter how small, the end results will not be as

satisfying as you hope.

Doing your best on every task does not mean making something seem more important than it really is, wasting time or forgetting your ultimate goal. Doing your best means making sure that every task you do receives the time and attention it deserves. It means taking the smallest jobs as seriously as the biggest jobs.

Dedicating an adequate amount of time and attention to each and every task you do will not slow you down. In fact, it can help you be better motivated for each task that awaits you. When you give your best to everyone, no matter how small, it increases your chances of being completely satisfied with the end results when you reach your most important goals.

17. About your co-workers and employees

There is a trend that is popular in today's business world. Some people believe that competition is the best way to increase productivity. No matter what line of work you are in, this approach is likely to backfire.

First, teamwork is much better than competition. When you use the approach that everyone works for the common good of the company, more will be achieved. When the sense of competition is eliminated, each person will want to contribute as much as possible simply because it is their place to do so. You will not feel that you have to outperform your co-workers, which in turn will increase the sense of teamwork. When everyone works as a team and works towards a common goal, productivity will increase.

Second, everyone needs to feel that they value it. This is as true in the workplace as anywhere else. The best employee, and the employee who does the most, is the one who believes that his or her work is appreciated.

Another factor in increasing productivity is reducing the amount of stress, friction and conflict in the workplace.

When there are employees who do not get along with others, or someone else does the work for them, or it is simply difficult to be around this or these people on a regular basis, these types of problems should be addressed as quickly as possible.

Productivity is best in the workplace where everyone gets along. This does not mean wasting time with unnecessary conversations and visits. Simply recognizing that everyone is there for the same purpose is usually enough.

The workplace should be a place where every employee feels comfortable. It should be a place where everyone knows that their co-workers all have the same goals in mind. When each person knows that they are a valuable part of the company and a valuable part of the team, each person will feel more confident and be more productive.

18. Personal Stimulus

Encouraging yourself by rewarding yourself throughout an activity can be a good thing. Unfortunately, if approached in the wrong way, it can be more problematic than it is worth. If you think you owe yourself time off, special gifts or something else remarkable every time you accomplish something, you'll soon find yourself accomplishing very little. Instead of seeing it as a reward for a job well done, you may begin to feel that you are entitled to special rewards or favors for completing tasks that are within your scope of responsibility anyway.

This is why giving yourself little "extras" to do your job is usually not a good idea. It is even more negative if you expect special recognition or rewards from your boss or co-workers for doing what you are supposed to do. Rewarding yourself as if you have achieved a spectacular achievement is not the best way to get the job done.

Instead, applying a little encouragement should be the only reward you need. When you complete a task on time, or do a project especially well, you can recognize it as a small but important success. When you apply this kind of encouragement with a figurative pat on the back, you reward yourself for a job well done. You'll also be ready to move on to the next task or step.

This concept works equally well whether you work alone or in a group. If no one feels compelled to believe that they should get some kind of special recognition for doing their job, the priority will be to get the job done. In work environments that include a number of people working together as a group, no one will feel more or less important than anyone else. Each person will realize that he or she is expected to contribute something, without expecting to receive anything unique for doing so.

Encouraging yourself along the way will serve to keep your spirits up and your sense of motivation at its peak. While major accomplishments may result in some small additional reward, personal encouragement should be the only reward needed to do your job.

19. Resist spreading yourself too thin

There are two ways you can go too far. You can do more work than you are reasonably capable of doing; or you can take on work that is beyond your capabilities. Both can overload your energy, make you feel frustrated, and discourage you a lot. They also result in being less productive.

You may know individuals who are addicted to work. These types of people, who continue to work even long after they have left the workplace, may feel that there is always something else they need to do, many hours after they have left the job. These subjects may feel that no work will be done or that it will not be done properly unless they are doing it themselves.

If you are this person, now is a good time to evaluate your over-extension habits. While you probably want to be conscientious and complete everything that is your responsibility, over-extending yourself will not make you more productive. It can have exactly the opposite effect.

Over-extending on a regular basis will exhaust you and wreak havoc on your health. Allowing yourself to get into this condition can affect your ability to concentrate.

You may begin to make unnecessary mistakes or be forgetful. You will not be able

to do as much as you had hoped.

You can resist overextending yourself by being reasonable with both your abilities and your time. Even if you are working on a very important project, you can't put "24/7" on it and expect it to go well.

You must take reasonable time to rest, eat, and exercise, and even some recreation, to be in the best condition to do the job.

Overextending yourself when trying to do a job that is beyond your capabilities can also be counterproductive. If you're not fully qualified to do it, it won't work. Instead of overextending yourself with something you know you can't do, it's better to leave it to someone who is actually qualified to

complete it properly.

Getting discouraged about your work doesn't have to happen. If you make it a point not to try too hard, you'll be more productive than if you try to take it all on yourself.

20. Why you need to de-stress

Stress has many results, and none of them are positive. The results of stress can get in the way of work. Even if a job is completed, the results of stress can minimize your sense of accomplishment and satisfaction. When you de-stress, you will do your best and appreciate the result.

Since each person is an individual, it may be helpful for you to determine the best ways to de-stress. A coffee break, a brisk walk, or thinking about something completely different for a few minutes are some ways that may be helpful to you. Your own personality and individual needs should be the deciding factors. A method that works for one person does not necessarily work as well for the next.

If you don't take off your stress when you need to, you won't do much. Stress can take away your concentration, leaving you to focus on anything other than the task at hand. Too much stress, especially if it's prolonged, can lead to fatigue and physical illness. In addition to causing headaches and a general feeling of malaise, prolonged stress even has the power to weaken your immune system. In the worst case, extreme and prolonged stress can lead to medical complications.

When stress has the power to cause all these problems, it should be easy to see how it can affect your work. That's why de-stressing when it's necessary shouldn't be considered a luxury, a nonsense, or a waste of time.

De-stressing should not be seen as an excuse. Once you have begun to assess the effects of stress on your work life, it should not be difficult to determine when the need to eliminate stress arises. However, neither you nor your job can afford to use de-stressing as an excuse to be lazy or irresponsible. A short break for whatever specific type of anti-stress method is most appropriate for you should reduce or alleviate your stress. When you are not overwhelmed by stress, it will be easier to concentrate on what you are doing and do it.

21. Establishing and classifying your priorities

When you're at work, pretty much everything you do is important. However, setting and ranking your priorities will help keep everything in its proper perspective. This is a positive way to do things.

Setting and prioritizing means recognizing that some tasks require more time than others, and some tasks require more work than others. If you make the mistake of trying to allocate the same amount of time to each task, you will slow down and not accomplish as much as you should.

While you want to do your best on each task, determining which ones will require more time and effort is a much more productive approach than trying to see everything as it is.

Setting and ranking your priorities also means determining which tasks need to be completed first. You may realize that this is only logical, but it often doesn't happen that way. There may be a very large project on the horizon that will require a significantly greater amount of time and effort than the smaller projects you have on hand. Perhaps there is one that includes a significant time period, or even a deadline. In cases like these, you may have been tempted to do the smaller, easier tasks first.

When you rank your priorities, you can start

by deciding which work or project needs your attention first. This method will not only ensure that it gets done, but also that you accomplish it without sufficient motivation to do it correctly. Similar to what was said earlier in this book about taking on the toughest jobs first, the sooner you start one with a deadline, the more likely you are to complete it on time.

Setting and ranking your priorities is not a difficult or time-consuming task. If you start each work day with a brief summary of everything you need to accomplish, you can assign top priority to the tasks that need to be completed first. Your entire workday will be much smoother and you'll be able to do more.

 PRODUCTIVITY 23 POWERFUL TIPS

22. Exercise good communication skills

Whether you work alone or in a busy office, good communication skills should be a standard part of your daily work life. The better you know how to develop these skills, the more you will be able to do. In turn, everyone you work with can be more productive.

Some people should be reminded that good communication skills include knowing the difference between successful communication and pointless time. You may have someone in your office who likes to "visit" co-workers all day long, or always seems to be talking on the phone. This type of social activity is not appropriate for the workplace. It prevents the work from being done.

Good communication skills in the workplace can generally be summarized into two categories. There is the type of communication that should be as direct, brief as possible. You can say what you need to say, ask a question or clarify something, without wasting your own time or that of the other person. The other type of communication involves giving, receiving or exchanging information. You may need to inform someone about an aspect of your work or ask for a detailed explanation of a project. In most cases, these are the only forms of communication that improve the workplace and increase productivity.

Good communication skills also involve being responsive and listening to what the other person is saying. Simply waiting your turn to speak is a negative habit that should have been eliminated in childhood. If you have not yet developed the habit of having good listening skills, it may be helpful to practice this habit during your free time. If you occasionally eat lunch or take a break with your co-workers, this can be an excellent time to develop your listening skills. Practicing good communication skills in the workplace saves time. When questions, answers and explanations are fully received when you first speak, the need for repetition is eliminated. It also gives the other person the message that what you say is valuable. When everyone is "on the same page," everyone will do more.

23. Strategies are appropriate everywhere!

When you hear the word "productivity," the first thing that comes to mind is probably your job and the workplace. The good news is that all of these strategies for increasing productivity are also appropriate for other "places" in life. They are just as useful for students who want to do more with their work in college or high school, and even for housewives who never seem to have enough time to do everything that needs to be done.

There are only twenty-four hours in a day. This is equally true for everyone. In the interest of your overall health and well-being, a number of those hours should be allocated for sleep, recreation, and other important health-related habits. While this still leaves plenty of hours in the day to get things done, your time can be misdirected or wasted if you allow it, or if you are unsure how best to manage those hours.

Strategies for getting things done focus on how best to manage your work hours for optimal productivity. When you learn how not to waste time and make the most of every hour and every day, you'll do more. In most cases, these are the only forms of communication that improve the workplace and increase productivity.

Good communication skills also involve being responsive and listening to what the other person is saying. Simply waiting your turn to speak is a negative habit that should have been eliminated in childhood. If you have not yet developed the habit of having good listening skills, it may be helpful to practice this habit during your free time.

Visit our author page on Amazon and get more **MENTES LIBRES!**

http://amazon.com/author/menteslibres

If you wish, you can leave a comment on this book by clicking on the following link so that we can continue to grow! Thank you very much for your purchase!

https://www.amazon.com/dp/B084RKRBLK

www.ingramcontent.com/pod-product-compliance
Lightning Source LLC
Chambersburg PA
CBHW050253220526
45465CB00002B/660